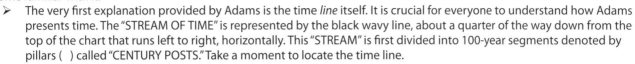
WHERE DO I START?

Adams' companion work to his chart is the *Key to Adams' Synchronological Chart*. This "Key" will be helpful to have your chart and key in front of you as you read this. Here is an overview of the "Key" to help you become familiar with it:

- ➤ The very first explanation provided by Adams is the time *line* itself. It is crucial for everyone to understand how Adams presents time. The "STREAM OF TIME" is represented by the black wavy line, about a quarter of the way down from the top of the chart that runs left to right, horizontally. This "STREAM" is first divided into 100-year segments denoted by pillars ( ) called "CENTURY POSTS." Take a moment to locate the time line.
  - o For practice, try finding the birth of Christ at the "0" century post. This is the dividing line denoting the start of the Christian Era. Thus, A.D. are the years from the start of the Christian Era and B.C. are the years before the Christian Era. The Explanatory Notes by the editor in Ussher's *The Annals of the World* offer a cogent discussion of the history of time.
  - o Now find 476 B.C. If this is a bit harder, see the next bullet.
- ➤ 100-year segments needed further divisions to be useful to Adams and others using the chart. Using red lines that run on the vertical axis (top to bottom) to the "STREAM OF TIME," Adams divides the centuries into decade or 10-year segments. When needed, Adams sub-divides the decade into single years with shorter red lines.
  - o Find the decade of A.D. 1580–1590. Above the "STREAM OF TIME" you will find an example of a decade divided into ten yearly increments.
  - o Look above the divided years and you will see an illustration that shows Shakespeare reading to Queen Elizabeth.
  - o Looking just immediately below the time-line you'll see that Shakespeare and Galileo (famous scientist) were alive at the same time.
- ➤ Below the "STREAM OF TIME" Adams starts a new stream for nation states as they arise and gives you each of the nations' rulers whose reigns are denoted by differing colors. The nation-state streams merge when one nation conquers another. Nation-states are re-established when they become independent of another's control.
  - o Locate the Tower of Babel; it is at this point that the different nations arise.
  - o Look between century posts 38 and 39 as the Roman Empire grows and begins to gobble up other nations.

The next section of the *Key* is Bible and Jewish History. This is the very first part of the chart, starting at the far left or, rather, with the first panel. It continues for the 3,607 years of Bible history.

1ˢᵗ Corn-Mill.

- ➤ Note that the Century Posts have numbers above and below each post up through the birth of Jesus. The numbers above denote years that have passed, times 100 (6 x 100 = 600 years) since the beginning of creation. These numbers (representing time) are counting up.
- ➤ The numbers below each post are the years B.C. based on the Christian Era. The numbers count down toward the birth of Jesus Christ, the Savior.
- ➤ With the birth of Jesus, (post #4004) the time B.C. becomes A.D. and numbering of the posts starts over above each post with post #1 (100) A.D. through 18 (A.D. 1800), where Adams stops recording.

Conjectural: Illustrating civilization of Stone age.

An excellent exercise would be to go through and locate the different ages — Antediluvian Period, the Patriarchal Age, the Mosaic Age — as presented in Adams' *Key*.

Adams next takes us on a historical journey, which he presents as highlighted on his chart. The natural divisions he observes are:

- ➤ GENEALOGY OF CHRIST
- ➤ THE FAMILY TREE (DELUGE TO MOSES)
- ➤ SUMMARY OF JEWISH POLITICAL HISTORY
- ➤ THE BABYLONISH CAPTIVITY

This is a well-written, concise history that Adams presents. Given his brevity, to read this with the chart by your side would present an amazing foundational big picture of biblical times.

Adams next presents Profane History (profane being secular or nonreligious) using nation-states as the basis for sketching the history of the world through the 1800s. The countries are visited in the order they appear:

- ➤ PHOENICIA, OR CANAAN
- ➤ EGYPT

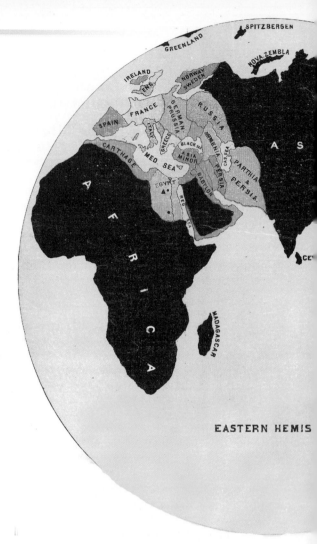

- CHALDEA, OR BABYLON
- PERSIA
- MEDIA
- THE PERSIAN EMPIRE
- NEW EMPIRE OF PERSIA
- GREECE
- MACEDONIAN EMPIRE
- SYRIA, UNDER THE SELEUCIDAE
- ITALY
- ROME
  - FIRST TRIUMVIRATE
  - SECOND TRIUMVIRATE
- PARTHIA
- BRITAIN
- THE SAXON HEPTARCHY (OR) OCTARCHY ESTABLISHED
- ENGLAND
- CHINA
- FRANCE (Gaul) AND GERMANY
- FRANCE
- SCOTLAND OR CALEDONIA
- NETHERLANDS
- POLAND
- RUSSIA
- DENMARK, SWEEDEN AND NORWAY
- PORTUGAL
- SPAIN
- ARABIAN OR SARACEN EMPIRE
- TURKEY OR THE OTTOMAN EMPIRE
- JAPAN
- THE UNITED STATES OF AMERICA
- IRELAND – THE EMERALD ISLE
- SWITZERLAND – HELVETIA

Switzerland concludes the historical synopsis of the Key. The next section, FOUND AT LAST, is a veritable Who's Who of Adams' day, each of whom praises Adams and the chart.

Lastly is a section called DESCRIPTION (author unknown) , which gives a description and some rather glowing commentary about the chart.

ACTIVITIES USING YOUR *Adams' Chart of History*:
This section of this guide will give you suggestions and example activities/lesson plans to get you started with this amazing resource. Whether home, church, homeschool, or school, you should find that the *Chart of History* begs your attention. **Across the grades and across the curriculum, teachers treasure the value of time-lines.**

1. PRIME THE PUMP
Without any introduction, fanfare, or comment, put up the time-line. The size, color, and uniqueness make the chart impossible to ignore. So my first suggestion is to simply put the chart where your family, class, or even you can easily see it.

The questions may start immediately. "What's this?" someone may ask, to which you reply, "Oh, it's a time-line." Let them look. Let them explore. If your lesson for the day is on a certain period covered in the chart, use a post-it to mark that time, person, event, or invention. Let them make the connection. Once that happens, set the hook a little deeper by asking, "What else was going on at that time?"

Lifelong learning is driven by a natural curiosity about life and all that goes on around us. Curiosity is an essential ingredient for inspired learning that often diminishes as students get older. School often becomes more about the finished product produced rather than the spark that ignited a creative journey. *Adams' Chart of History* is a welcome tool to continue or re-ignite the fire of curiosity.

2. WHO AM I?

Any history is a history about people and the times and events that shape them. Biographical studies can work in two directions. One way is to have the student find someone on *Adams' Chart* and have the student research that person. The other direction is to combine literature or Bible studies in the form of biographies or autobiographies and then have the student locate the person's time on the *Adams' Chart*.

Once the person or his or her time is located, ask your student to scan the century before to develop a sense of what preceded and shaped this person's life. Were there any natural occurrences (earthquake? flood?) that affected the person? Were there any people or major works of literature, art, or invention that impacted the person? What was the political climate of the time? Who was alive at the same time that may have been a major influence for the person's thoughts, feelings, and/or actions? Develop more questions in your discussions with your student or class.

3. WE ARE FAMILY

Learning about our own family history is a natural motivator for most students. Use the time-line to look at Adam and Eve's family. Then look at Noah's family. There are activities that can flow from the study of family groups on the *Adams' Chart*.

- ➤ Have the students create a time-line of the last 100 years. Using post-it, pushpins with flags, or index cards and tape, locate the birth (and death, where applicable) of family members going back to great-grandfathers/mothers. Younger students may want to only go back as far as grandparents using a time-line of only 50 years. You may want to ask:
    - ○ How do life spans in your family compare to those in Adam and Eve's family? How long did Methuselah live?
    - ○ How do life spans compare before the Flood with those today?
    - ○ Develop your own questions.
- ➤ You have an outline with the information on births and deaths. What else might you add?
    - ○ Where they lived, or when they moved.
    - ○ Inventions that impacted their lives.
    - ○ Major events in the world right on down to their community that affected them.

Primitive Spinning and Weaving.

This may naturally lead to questions involving the Higher Order Thinking Skills (H.O.T.S.) of Bloom's Taxonomy (see Appendix A). Analysis, synthesis, and evaluation all require a higher order of thinking than fact-based information. With the above information, you are ready to look for cause/effect relationships for decisions made by people in your very own family. What does this mean for you and your family? An example might be to ask, "How did decisions of author Laura Wilder's *(Little House on the Prairie)* parents help make her who she became?"

4. ALL THE NEWS

Use a moment in history as a reference point to have your students create a newspaper.

- ➤ Choose the town, nation/state where the paper is published.
- ➤ Choose the point of view for the paper. Are you mine workers publishing a paper in support of your efforts to unionize, or do the owners of the mine own the paper? Are you the recorder for Nimrod and the builders of the Tower of Babel writing about the tragedy of God's intervention, or the lone paper reporting what happens when we refuse to allow God to guide our paths?
- ➤ Choose a name for your paper that reflects your perspective.
- ➤ One student can write an article or the whole paper, or a class can be divided into editors/reporters responsible for different story assignments: one could interview the locals for their reaction; another could report the official line of the rulers; yet another could examine the situation from a unique perspective (business, medical, restaurant, etc.).
- ➤ For fun, be sure to add classified or display ads, a gossip column, and the like. This is a great opportunity to learn or imagine what life was like at a personal level. It's why presidential candidates are asked, "How much does a gallon of milk or loaf of bread sell for?"

5. IS THERE A DOCTOR IN THE HOUSE?

Actually, you can substitute lawyer, inventor, mathematician, etc., for IS THERE A _____ IN THE HOUSE, so be inventive.

- ➤ Using *Exploring The History of Medicine* by John Hudson Tiner from Master Books (www.masterbooks.net), we will locate and describe the contributions of each person as they helped advance the care and treatment of patients.
- ➤ Read Chapter 1: The First Physicians.
- ➤ Find and flag with push-pin or post-it
    - ○ Imhotep, after 2242 B.C.
    - ○ Hippocrates, after 2243 B.C.

- o Galen, A.D. 200
- ➤ Continue on to locate people and their accomplishments as you read the book.
  - o Why are there large gaps of time in the beginning?
  - o Galen wrote a lot of books on medicine, 80 of which still survive today. What was the impact, good or bad, of Galen's writing?
  - o Rank the top three people whose contributions resulted in the most/best advancements. Be able to support your choices with logic, reasoning, and evidence.

6. FOR THE BIBLE TELLS ME SO

The written word becomes much more real when a student actually locates a biblical event on the time-line. Many people will appreciate the BIG PICTURE that lets us concretely see the progression of people and events. We tend to more easily see the truth of God's Word.

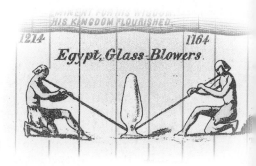

Let's start with some easy ones:
- ➤ Locate the Deluge (Flood) on the chart (2348 B.C.)
- ➤ The illustration below the Deluge shows the ark on Mt. Ararat. What are the dimensions given?
- ➤ Locate the birth of Methuselah (3317 B.C.). What year did he die? How long had he lived? Whose son was he?

A bit harder:
- ➤ Methuselah's life overlapped Adam's life. They spoke together for 243 years. What is the importance of this in terms of history? What is the significance of the "two pillars" found in the illustration just below the century posts of 15 and 16? What nations existed before the Tower of Babel? What was wrong with Nimrod's leadership that God would do what He did? What nations develop immediately following the Tower of Babel?
  - o To extend your learning, look at the illustrations of the Rosetta Stone and the Moabite Stone at the bottom of panel three. Why are these stones needed? What purpose did the stones serve?
  - o Using the chart of language at the bottom of panel 4, write your name in hieroglyphics, in Greek, and in Hebrew.
  - o Have you ever tried to communicate with someone who is speaking in another language and who does not speak or understand your language? Describe the problems you had communicating.
- ➤ Consider having your students locate the time or person on the *Adams' Chart*. Post or pin the Bible verse so that they begin to get a sense of how it all fits together.

As you can readily see, the *Adams' Chart* can be the impetus of many discussions and teachings. It can also be a great resource for reference work.

Methuselah talked with Adam 243 years learning the worlds history from the beginning. He wrote it on these two Pillars or "Books." Moses had access to these "Books."
Josephus.

A Panel-by-Panel Overview

Now that you have a firm foundation for how the time-line works and flows, let's start at the beginning and look at people, places, and things, panel by panel.

First Panel: 4004 B.C. to 3800 B.C. and
Second Panel: 3800 B.C. to 3500 B.C.

"In the beginning God . . . ." The chart begins with God's creation. The date is accurate as determined by Archbishop Ussher (also spelled Usher) and published in 1658 in his classic book, *The Annals of the World*. Adams explains that Moses assigns no date, and then wonders, "How long after this 'beginning,' before the history of man begins is unknown."

However, from a plain reading of the first chapter of Genesis, we know that the time from the "beginning" until the history of man begins is a matter of days, not long periods of time. Genesis 1 is clear that God created the heavens and earth in six actual days, each approximately 24 hours long. God created the first two humans on Day 6 of that first week. For more information, see www.answersingenesis.org/go/genesis.

Although Adams seems to leave open the possibility that the histories of other cultures may extend far beyond the 4004 BC date given by Ussher, we know that all ethnic groups are descended from Adam and Eve. So any chronology must be reconciled with the Bible's accurate account of history. For more information, see www.answersingenesis.org/go/history.

"Adam is the first man found in any history," and the challenge is made for anyone with anything different to step forward. As God's written record of history, the Bible holds the true account of history from the very beginning. Adams has chosen to begin his time-line with the first man, Adam.

These two panels contain the rationale for starting with Adam.

The information at the top of the page also contains some factual data as to how many books are in the Bible and authorship.

The genealogy of Adam and Eve, and indeed of the human race, is next. This flows from left to right and continues until 721 B.C. (Panel #12) when the ten tribes of Israel are carried away by Shalmaneser into Assyria, thus becoming the "Lost Tribes" and marking the end of the Kingdom of Israel (see p. 80 in *The Annals of the World*). The Kingdom of Judah continues until 588 B.C., thus marking the "End of Jewish Independence" when they were "scattered" (Panel # 12).

"The long black line (that) represents the stream of time" is next. It is divided by pillars into periods of 100 years. The numbers at the top of the pillars are the centuries from the creation of Adam (3= 300; 4=400, etc.). As you see, the centuries count up to the birth of Jesus. The numbers under each pillar count down and are the centuries B.C. (Before Christ), or Before the Common Era (B.C.E.), as it is sometimes denoted today.

Below the actual time-line you will see "Adam 130." This is Adam's name followed by his age when his son Seth was born. Then you see "Seth 105," 105 being Seth's age when Enos was born. This continues through Joseph. These lines represent the genealogy of Christ.

Below Christ's genealogy line is an illustration of Cain and Abel. To the right and below that is more explanation of the Chart. The Eastern Hemisphere map is pictured to bolster Adams' hope that the Chart will be an "indispensable adjunct" in teaching geography.

If possible, find or buy a world map to put on the wall or a bulletin board. Generally you can find one that is about 3 feet by 2 feet. This can be an indispensable aid for learning, and to truly get the big picture. Refer to the map often as you look at the time-line to establish a sense of time and place. Keep in mind, however, that the "world that then was" perished in the Flood of Noah's day. So the geography of today's world is different from the geography of the pre-Flood world. Today's maps don't reflect the world that Adam lived in. For more information, see the Rodinia Wall Chart, available from answersbookstore.com.

Note that Adams does not give a date for Abel being slain, nor does Adams guess at when certain personages died. He makes note of such as "unknown" and will often indicate this with a question mark symbol. Also note that Adams often gives a biblical reference with comments or illustrations, such as "Gen. 4c. 8v." for the "Death of Abel."

The Second Panel also illustrates some of the tools of the Stone Age (the "1st Corn-Mill"). However, keep in mind that the various "ages" (Stone Age, Bronze Age, Iron Age) weren't distinct periods of time, but rather descriptions of the tools used by a certain group of people in a certain location. So, for example, one people group (descendants from those separated at Babel) may have been more adept at using tools made from stone, while other groups had acquired (or kept) the knowledge of working with metals.

Adams also provides some of the "Eminent Historians" he consulted. Below that, at the bottom of the panel, is a list of the "Books consulted in this work."

Look at the list of "Eminent Historians" listed by Adams. How many do you recognize? Look up at least three of the historians in an encyclopedia or online. Take notes to give an oral report to someone in your family.

Read the list of books Adams consulted in creating the time-line. Have you heard of any of these? Tell why you think this is — why, why not?

Third Panel: 3500 B.C. to 3200 B.C.
The statement at the top of this panel speaks to the "Many discoveries and inventions . . ." that came from the artisans and artistry of Cain's descendents.

Read Genesis 4:20–22. Using what you read and what you see at the top left of panel three, write a list of the children of Lamech and their areas of expertise.

To extend your study: Adams calls one of the sons of Lamech "The 'VULCAN' of the Greeks." Look up the historical reference and then describe what the statement means.

"The Patriarchal Age," according to Adams, is 4004 B.C. to 1491 B.C., the date when the "Law of Moses" is given. This is different than the patriarchal age reported in the Torah that begins with the receding waters of the Flood. Hebrew histories will sometimes place the "Age" beginning with Abraham. Others consider Genesis 11:27–Exodus 18:27 the Patriarchal Age.

The genealogy of Adam and Eve continues above the actual time-line, as does the genealogy of Christ below the time-line. Below Christ's genealogy are illustrations of "Stone Age" implements that continue from the second panel. Note that the life of the longest living person, Methuselah, begins in 3317 B.C.

> *When was the "Stone Age"?*

> *Reading the paragraph between the illustration of the "1st Corn-Mill" and the "Inferred" maps, what does Adams mean when he states, "It would seem unnecessary to hunt for fabulous antiquity"?*

The map located on the left-hand side of the panel is drawn from the Scripture of Genesis 10. Adams appropriately states the map is "inferred" as there are no known maps from this period.

> *Compare this map in panel three with your map of the current world. Do any of the places on the "Inferred" map still exist today?*

> *What is meant by "The Ends of the Earth" in the panel three map?*

> *Draw a map from your house to your local library.*

To the right of the map is a "Babylonian Brick" of ancient Chaldea showing a cuneiform inscription. To the right of this is a text block that promotes Adams' format for the time-line. Below this is a "Scripture Chronology," the text of which explores creation, matter, and time. A comment from Dr. John Eadie (1810-1876), a Glasgow minister ordained in 1835, is included.

Below the map, one sees the continuation of the "Eminent Historians" consulted in making of the chart.

The middle and bottom right positions of the third panel are occupied by two illustrations and descriptions of the Rosetta Stone and the Moabite Stone. These ancient specimens aided in the deciphering, understanding, and appreciation of ancient languages.

> *The history of these stones is fascinating. Where are they today?*

> *View http://www.christiananswers.net/dictionary/moabitestone.html.*
> *The inscription on the Moabite Stone, in a remarkable degree, supplements and corroborates the history of King Mesha recorded in 2 Kings 3:4-27. What do they say?*

> *What is another name for the Moabite Stone?*

Fourth Panel: 3200 B.C. to 2900 B.C.
The writing at the top right of panel four and crossing into the top left of panel five points out that the entirety of history of 2,553 years could have been passed "from creation to Moses's death" with only five links.

> *Looking at the lineage of Adam, can you arrive at fewer than five links to reach Moses?*

The line of Enoch ends and Adams' endnote states that he was an ". . . eminent astronomer, mathematician and prophet of God."

The genealogy of Adam and Eve continues above the actual time-line, interspersed with information on marriage, intermarriage, and Seth's family. Adams comment on brother-sister intermarriage addresses the old question, "Who was Cain's wife?" For more information, see www.answersingenesis.org/go/cains-wife.

Adams says that 125 pounds of silver was worth $1,500 and 125 pounds of gold was worth $24,000. The amount would have been determined with prices from the mid-1800s.

How many ways can you use to find out the value of gold and silver today? Make a chart showing how you could research this question.

What would 125 pounds of silver and/or gold be worth in today's market? (Try figuring this without a calculator.)

The genealogy of Christ is below the time-line with Lamech.

The left side of panel four has a column related to "Pictorial Language" and, at the bottom, "Egyptian Hieroglyphic Letters." The center column looks at the origins of "Alphabetic Language."

Write your name using hieroglyphics and ancient Greek symbols.

The bottom half of the middle column and the middle of the right column of panel four are filled with succinct histories of ancient civilizations. Keep in mind that all of these civilizations began as descendants of Noah settled various places. For more information, visit www. answersingenesis.org/go/grandsons.

Also note Dr. Eadie's quote about Mesopotamia and the abode of men. Can we say for certain that Mesopotamia was the abode of men before the Flood? Remember, the Flood destroyed the "world that then was," so we wouldn't expect the topography of the earth to be the same as the pre-Flood world.

At the top of the right-hand column, located below the genealogy of Christ, you find the beginning of illustrations depicting Cain's descendants, showing that each family became known for certain skills. Many of these skills were carried with Noah and his family into the post-Flood world and passed on to their descendants. Other skills had to be redeveloped.

Fifth Panel: 2900 B.C. to 2600 B.C.
The genealogy of Adam and Eve continues above the actual time-line. At the top right of this panel Adams give the "years of History" covered by the Bible. Below "Jared," Adams begins the story of Noah and the ark.

Between the century posts, Adams tells of Methuselah.

IRON AGE
From TUBAL-CAIN.

Noah continues the genalogy of Christ. Below and to the left are the continued (from panel four) illustrations of Cain's descendants. Tubal-Cain is credited with beginning the Iron Age. The "Iron Age" mentioned in this panel refers to the pre-Flood time during which Tubal-Cain learned to work with metals. Because of the destructive nature of the Flood, we wouldn't necessarily expect to find many artifacts from this time. However, Tubal-Cain's knowledge may have been passed down through Noah to his descendants, or they may have redeveloped the knowledge on their own. These post-Flood artifacts (e.g., the daggers from Austria and the implements from Switzerland) are the ones found in various parts of the world today.

When was the Iron Age?

Why would the iron of the Iron Age have been an improvement over bronze?

The left and middle columns then continue the brief histories begun in panel four. Below these are the written accounts of the archeological findings of the "Sculptures from Nineveh." The "colossal stone Bulls" are wonderfully illustrated at the bottom of the left and middle columns.

Be sure to look up the Scripture 2 Kings 18:13–14. By reading the story inscribed on the ten bulls and by reading the Scripture, you will see the accuracy of the Bible as a historical document is verified.

What does it mean to be verified?

The right side of panel five, beginning in the middle, relates "Traditions respecting the Tower of Babel," and Adams' observations as to the validity of the actual tower.

Below the Tower of Babel piece are the writings outlining "The Seven Wonders of the World." Who developed this list is unknown, but it is a generally accepted list for the ancient world that Adams gives. Below the title he encourages us to "see illustrations."

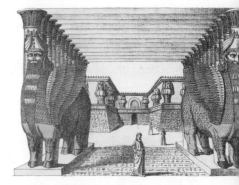

Find the illustrations of the seven different wonders.

What do the wonders have in common? How do they differ?

What would be your top seven for today's world?

Sixth Panel: 2600 B.C. to 2300 B.C.
The Deluge or Noah's deluge, commonly known as the Flood, occurs on this panel. Methuselah dies before the Flood. The Deluge erases the corruptness of man by erasing mankind, leaving only the eight souls of Noah and his family to be saved.

How long was Noah's family in the ark?

Illustrations below the genealogy of Christ include "First Navigators," "Primitive Spinning and Weaving," and "Agriculture during the iron age." Below this is "Noah, his 3 Sons, and their Posterity, " an interesting delineation by Adams of the "Scattered Families of Mankind."

Look up and write the definition of primitive, navigator, delineation, posterity, and ethnology.

The right side of panel six is taken with the rainbow and its promise, and an illustration of the ark on Ararat. For more on the shape of the Ark, visit www.answersingenesis.org/go/noahs-ark.

At the bottom right of the panel is the "Peoples of the World." The idea of five different "races" of people is contrary to the biblical teaching that there is only one race—the human race. We are all related—descended from Adam and Eve, and more recently, through Noah and his family. The five races idea also runs counter to current scientific findings that genetic differences between people groups are very miniscule. For more information, see www.answersingenesis.org/go/racism.

Of special note is the illustration of Methuselah, Noah, and Shem standing before two pillars, one of brick and one of stone, whereupon Methuselah, with his 243 years of talking with Adam, has recorded the world's history. However, think about this statement concerning the two pillars: they "stood in Moses time 777 years after." If the pillars were erected before the Flood, how could they have survived the Flood (which covered the whole earth)? The only possible way is that Noah took the pillars on the Ark and then deposited them somewhere after he came off the Ark. Of course, there is no actual biblical evidence for this speculation; rather, this is based on the supposition of Josephus.

The statement that Moses had access to the pillars or books is most important, given that Moses is the author of Genesis. For more information, see the section "Who really wrote Genesis?" at www.answersingenesis.org/go/genesis.

Think about and then explain to someone else why the fact that Moses knew of Methuselah's pillars is so important.

Who was Josephus?

Seventh Panel: 2300 B.C. to 2000 B.C.
This panel starts at the top with the "Confusion of Tongues" in 2247 B.C., which results in the "Dispersion." This is the Tower of Babel event (Gen. 11) that is pictured on the left side of the panel.

The genealogy of Adam and Eve continues with the multiplying of Noah's family. Make note of the diminishing years lived by the descendents of Noah's children. For more information, see the section on life spans at www.answersingenesis.org/go/genetics.

Be sure to read between the lines, It's there you will find that Nimrod is the founding father of Babylon. Below the genealogy of Christ one sees that the confusion of tongues leads to the dispersion of the families around the world and begins the rise of nation-states.

What are the five countries pictured in 2000 B.C. on the right side of panel seven?

Adams offers numerous tidbits of history and previews of things to come in the rest of the panel. Illustrations of costumes, ancient Egyptian architecture, and Greek gods are presented. The science of geometry has its beginnings.

Eighth Panel: 2000 B.C. to 1700 B.C.
This panel takes us to the end of the 2,369 years covered by the Book of Genesis. This is the time of Abraham, Rebekah, Sodom and Gomorrah (1898 B.C.), Jacob, and Joseph. They are all here.

There are many biblical references in panel eight. The call of Abraham (Abram) takes place in 1921 B.C. (Gen. 12).

The genealogy of Adam and Eve continues above the time-line. The genealogy of Christ continues below the time-line. Below this are illustrations of Sodom and Gomorrah (Gen. 19), Abraham's trial (Gen. 22 in 1871 B.C.), Rebekah (Gen. 24 in 1856 B.C.), Jacob's ladder (Gen. 28:12 in 1779 B.C.), Bethel "House of God" (Gen. 28:18), and "Joseph's Dream."

Below the biblical event illustrations are the nation-state time-lines, presented with a different color for each ruler in the line of the nation. Often Adams includes comments within the line about the ruler or an event that happened during their reign. In the space between the nation's time-lines of panel eight are illustrations of architecture, life, dress, etc., for Phoenicia, Egypt, Babylon, and Greece. The time-line for China runs along the bottom of the chart. For more information on the technological advances of ancient peoples, see www.answersingenesis.org/go/history.

Note that Adams gives Abraham his own time-line that cleverly reflects his movement from Babylon to Canaan to Egypt. The line morphs to Isaac, Joseph, and Jacob so the student can visually see the movements of these families.

The bottom 20 percent of this panel is devoted primarily to the ancient history of Egypt. However, there are many problems with Manetho's chronology of Egypt. For more information on the attempts to reconcile biblical and Egyptian chronologies, see the relevant articles at www.answersingenesis.org/go/history.

Ninth Panel: 1700 B.C. to 1400 B.C.
The Book of Genesis ends to be followed by the Books of Exodus, Leviticus, Numbers, Deuteronomy, and the sixth book, Joshua, all of which cover events of this time period. Judges, the seventh book, begins. Adams shifts from the genealogy of Adam and Eve to following the kingdom of Israel in the space above the time-line. This is the time of Moses.

Below "Exodus, 145" (145 being the years covered) are the "10 Plagues"; "3 Great Events"; and "3 Great Changes." A brief review of the list of "Plagues" certainly leads one to count his or her blessings.

Try to imagine a plague of frogs! Or boils and blains! And what is "Murrain"? See http://www. christiananswers.net/dictionary/murrain.html.

The illustrations between the century posts are of Job, the "Burning Bush," and Moses at "Horeb." Under the time-line of the genealogy of Christ are illustrations of Jacob and his family going into Egypt, the Golden Calf, the Brazen Serpent (Exod. 7:8), the Law given of Sinai (Lev. 26:46), and the Altar of Burnt Offerings (Exod. 38).

Between the time-line of Phoenicia and Egypt you can see the travels of Moses, including his 40 years in the wilderness and his death. The time-line of rulers for Phoenicia splits as Joshua leads the Israelites into the land God promised, identified here as Palestine.

This panel introduces two new nation-states with Lydia of Asia Minor and Italy (Latium). In 1550 B.C., the chart shows Lydia splitting with the rise of Troy (Ilium). Not yet fully formed, Greece is less nation-state than several city-states.

Of note are two small illustrations, one of Atlas and the other of a flute. More ancient Greek history is found written above and below the China time-line.

Tenth Panel: 1400 B.C. to 1100 B.C.
This panel covers the Book of Judges (begun in the ninth panel), the Book of Ruth, and the better part of 1 Samuel. In the illustration at the top of this panel Adams even spells out the Judges and the years of their reign. Samson, a well-known story from the Bible, is among the Judges.

Below the line of rulers for Babylon and Assyria is the line of rulers of Asia Minor. Look to the left to find one ruler who became a character of myth, Midas.

The message in the story of Midas and his golden touch makes it worth re-visiting. How do myths begin?

Is there any truth to the story of Midas?

The story of Midas continues as a myth involving donkey ears and Apollo. What is the point of the story?

Drawings above the time-line include the ark of the covenant. Those below the genealogy of Christ show articles from the Tabernacle. Other drawings to look for are the "Argonautic Expedition under Jason" (1263 B.C.) shown by a small vertical red bar, and the Trojan War, with a vertical red bar indicating all the Greek city-states involved.

Additionally, Adams notes the connection between several languages (Sanskrit, Persian, Greek, etc.). For more on how languages have developed from the original language families that resulted from the dispersion at Babel, see www. answersingenesis.org/go/linguistics.

Eleventh Panel: 1100 B.C. to 8000 B.C.
This busy, yet wonderfully laid out, panel takes us from the end of 1 Samuel through the Song of Solomon 22. Pictured are David and Goliath, Solomon, and Solomon's Temple. Below the Temple illustration are the ruling lines of the Kingdom of Israel and the Kingdom of Judah.

The time-line and genealogy of Christ continues. Below that, the time-line of rulers for Phoenicia, which split in 1451 B.C., shows what was Palestine in panel ten has become Judah in panel eleven. This line is duplicated above the century time-line for the duration of the Kingdom of Israel.

The depiction of the time-lines of rulers continues from left to right.

Note that Homer of Asia Minor and Solomon are contemporaries of their time. The birth of Zoroaster, the Persian philosopher, is 1082 B.C. — found on the left side of the panel. Also of note is the illustration of Romulus and Remus suckling the she wolf, thus marking the beginnings of Rome.

Twelfth Panel: 800 B.C. to 500 B.C.
Fourteen books of the Bible cover this time span. This is the time of Daniel, Nebuchadnezzar and his dream, the end of the Kingdom of Israel, the end of Jewish Independence, and the rise of the 229-year Persian Empire.

The upper right corner features the third wonder of the world, the Temple of Diana.

Between century posts 34 and 35 you see the illustration of "Mene, Tekel . . ." wherein Daniel reads the "writing on the wall."

What did the writing say?

What does to see the "writing on the wall" mean today?

What happened in 538 B.C. after Daniel read the writing on the wall to create that meaning?

How many years ago was this?

Solon (638 B.C., highlighted in red), one of the seven wise men of Greece, is featured about mid-panel, toward the right. His contemporaries include Pythagoras (math and philosophy, 571 B.C., highlighted in red), Aesop (620 B.C., highlighted in red) of fable fame, and Croesus — the last ruler of Lydia of Asia Minor, defeated by Cyrus.

The lower quarter of the panel features the first Olympiad in 776 B.C. at the left side. Looking to the lower right one can find Confucius of China. Other things to look for are the beginnings of Rome; the Roman Census; Thespis, the father of drama and acting; and the life (and unusual death) of Aeschylus, the dramatist.

Thirteenth Panel: 500 B.C. to 200 B.C.
This panel portrays the end of the 39 books of the Old Testament in 397 B.C. Above the "Stream of Time" time-line are the beasts of Daniel's visions, and illustrations of the fourth, fifth, sixth, and seventh Wonders of the World. One also sees the Alexandrian Library and Diogenes, the cynic.

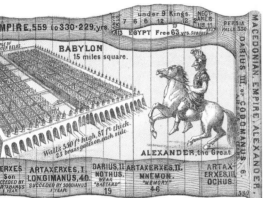

The profane history, viewed below the genealogy of Christ, is very active. A new nation, Caledonia, later and better known as Scotland, begins its march across time. At a glance you can see the breadth of the Persian Empire, its fall and the beginnings of the rise of the Roman Empire (in pink — third line up from the bottom). Many of the better known of the ancient Greek personages are featured from the golden age of Greece. One sees Plato, Socrates, Pindar, Demosthenes, Archimedes, Euclid, and Aristotle.

Look up Plato, Socrates, Pindar, Demosthenes, Archimedes, Euclid, and Aristotle.

Write a paragraph on each, explaining why their particular contribution has made them a lasting historical person.

For a brief span of time, Alexander III (the Great), who as a youth was tutored by Aristotle, rules much of the known world. With his death at age 33, the visual representation of rulers of the various nations goes from 7 to as many as 15.

> *The Persian Empire was one of historical significance.*
>
> *How long did it last?*
>
> *Who were its rulers?*
>
> *Why was Alexander III considered to be Alexander "the Great"?*

At the bottom right of the panel is the illustration of the Great Wall of China, built in a surprisingly short period of time.

> *How long did it take to build the Great Wall?*
>
> *How long was the Great Wall?*
>
> *What was the purpose for building the Great Wall?*

Fourteenth Panel: 200 B.C. to A.D. 100
At the top left of this chart, Adams reiterates the "Plan of the Chart." Below that is an overview of "Roman Government." Illustrations depicting Cleopatra, the Magi, and Jesus are found above the century time-line. The genealogy of Jesus comes to an end with his birth. The years of Jesus' life are proclaimed in gold. For more on the historicity of the life, death, and resurrection of Jesus Christ, see www.answersingenesis.org/go/Jesus-Christ.

The rise of the Roman Empire and Parthian Empire dominate the chart. Portraits of Roman luminaries, the Coliseum, Pompei, and Jerusalem are seen.

> *What nation-states are consumed by the Roman Empire?*
>
> *What nation or city-states are devoured by the Parthian Empire?*
>
> *What governments were not taken by either the Roman Empire or the Parthian Empire?*

Fifteenth Panel: A.D. 100 to 400
The top upper left of this panel is by an illustration of the Ptolemaic System, which features the earth as the center of the universe (i.e., all things revolve around the earth). Middle center at top is a fairly accurate map of the world drawn by Ptolemy.

Constantine's conversion to Christianity (A.D. 313) makes him the first Christian Emperor of the Roman Empire. In A.D. 325, Constantine calls for what will be the first Ecumenical Council, the result of which is the Nicene Creed. Marked by a red ring is the second Ecumenical Council (A.D. 351).

What does "ecumenical" mean?

What is the importance of the Nicene Creed?

Sixteenth Panel: A.D. 400 to 700

Above the time-line are illustrations of Celtic houses, Celts, the Saxon invasion of England, St. Patrick in Ireland (A.D. 432), Chariot of the Lazy Kings, the Mosque of Omar built on the spot of the razed Solomon's Temple includes a brief history of Jerusalem, and Cambridge University's founding is featured. Red-rimmed rings represent the third through sixth (Ecumenical) councils on this panel.

The "Chariot of the 'Lazy Kings' of France" is an odd name. Who are the "Lazy Kings"?

Why do you think Adams felt the "Lazy Kings" to be a "salient" fact of history, worthy of being included on the chart?

Who are Pepin and Charles Martel?

Below the time-line, Scotland and China continue on, but with the fall of the Roman Empire, one sees the re-emergence of nation-states. Some countries, like England, France, and Germany, struggle to find their identity and appear fragmented as various rulers fight for control of real estate.

We see the rise of Sarmatia, which will become Poland and Russia. You see the start of the ruling lineage for Scandinavia that will become Norway, Sweden, and Denmark. Ireland gets its own time-line starting in A.D. 597.

The plundering marauders, Alaric and Attila with his Huns, wreak havoc on Rome and Europe. The "Middle Ages" begin in A.D. 476 with the rise of the feudal system. Some of the remains of the Roman Empire are referred to as the Western Empire and others as the Greek or Eastern Empire.

The Koran is presented in 610, seen at the bottom middle of the panel. Beside the yellow and red scroll drawing of the Koran you can see how the rulers Omar and Othman in 21 years join Persia with Egypt, Palestine, and Arabia, creating the Saracen Empire. Charles Martel would stop the advance of the Saracen Empire at the Battle of Tours (see above left of the next panel).

Seventeenth Panel: A.D. 700 to 1000

On the top right of this panel, Adams presents a preview of things to come with his listing of the "Principal European Battles Since 1500." The upper left corner continues the written history briefs of Saxony and Bavaria (begun on panel sixteen). Below these historical vignettes begun on panel sixteen, Adams informs us about arithmetic, paper, and the first bank (808). These descriptions surround a drawing of Abraham's "Ka.a.ba or Temple." Below that is an illustration of Charles Martel defeating the Saracens at the Battle of Tours (732).

Look into the history of paper. Can you make your own paper? Try.

In the middle, above the time-line, you will see witches, a Caliph, "Otho the Great of Germany," and the "Feudal System." There is also a note regarding the founding of Oxford University (886).

FEUDAL SYSTEM.
Existed from the 7ᵗʰ to the 11ᵗʰ Century

What was the "Feudal System"?

What were the advantages for each class of people under the Feudal System?

This time is typically characterized as the "Middle Ages." Why?

Below the time-line are 300 years of active history. Scotland continues, as does Ireland. England (except Scotland) is finally united by Egbert. England struggles with France over Normandy. France, Germany, Spain, and Italy work to settle boundaries, while Prussia, Poland, Russia, Sweden, Denmark, and Norway establish their independence. Italy comes to terms with the Roman Catholic Church and the papal lineage is begun in A.D. 755.

The Greek or Eastern Empire remains fairly constant. The Saracen Empire lasts 314 years and falls in A.D. 936. With the fall, Egypt becomes independent once more. Adams continues China's chronology of rulers, but editorializes about the 12 unnamed emperors from A.D. 900 to 960, saying they were ". . . of no note."

Eighteenth Panel: A.D. 1000 to 1300
At the top of the panel, above the time-line, the "Treaties of Peace" are framed by illustrations on the left and the right. On the left are two knights jousting alongside a comment captioned "Chivalry." Below that are pictured a "Round Tower, the First Crusade" (Crusades are symbolized by red crosses between the lines of France and Austria), "King Canute," and "Knighthood." At the right top are "Magic Lanterns," the pillory, a London house of 1240, and a drawing of an open book tells us the when and by whom the Bible was divided into chapter and verse. Pictured is the Leaning Tower of Pisa with nearby cathedral. Immediately under the "Tower" is the notation "1220 Westminster Abbey Built," and to the right "Spectacles."

What is a "Crusade"?

When was the first Crusade?

What was the purpose of Crusades?

How many Crusades were there?

How many of those were successful?

Why did the Crusades stop?

The writing at the upper right includes a couple of notes of interest. The note about "Edward 1st" explains who becomes the "Prince of Wales." And "Windsor Castle" shows that even the history of a building can be interesting. Also, look between the #11 and #12 century posts to see the small flag emblazoned with 1066 as a reminder of the Battle of Hastings.

What is the historical significance of the Battle of Hastings?

KNIGHTHOOD
AND CHIVALRY EXISTED FROM THE 8th TO THE 15th CENTURY.

Thomas Becket and Roger Bacon, prominent historical personages, are featured just below the time-line. If you follow along the English line of rulers and read the short notes on most, you will see King John, who granted the Magna Charta in 1215.

The Magna Charta is one of the great historical and foundational documents of democracy.

What powers were limited for the rulers of England?

What rights were given to those being ruled?

There are eight Crusades symbolized by red crosses below the ruler time-line for France. There were six ecumenical councils held from 1130 to 1214, so noted by the writing inside the red rings in the time-line.

Also of note, looking at the bottom of the panel beginning around A.D. 1100 is the rise of the Mogul Empire and its most famous ruler, Genghis Khan or Zengis Khan.

Nineteenth Panel: A.D. 1300 to 1600
These are times of discovery and invention as Europe moves out of the Middle Ages. Above the time-line are illustrations of the mariner's compass (1302), gunpowder (1320), air guns and muskets (about 1400), playing cards (1382), chimneys and window glass (1300), pumps, the first watch, cannon (1308), hand cannon (1378), Gutenberg's press (about 1440), the spinning wheel (1530), and the Wickliffe's Bible and the Bishop's Bible are also pictured. Two-thirds down the panel on the right is an illustration of St. Peter's at Rome (commenced 1506).

Pick one of the above inventions. Research, prepare, and present a three-minute informative speech about your chosen invention.

You will recognize the likes of William Tell (1306), Joan of Arc (1431), Martin Luther (1521), Queen Elizabeth, William Shakespeare, Erasmus, Thomas Wolsey, Galileo, Sir Edward Coke, King Ferdinand and Queen Isabella, Henry the Eighth of England's break with the Catholic Church, the War of the Roses, Spain's becoming a super power of its day, the coming of age (1462) of the czars of Moscow, and the Ottoman-Empire or Turkey.

Why did Henry the Eighth want to break with the Catholic Church?

Memorize a poem written by William Shakespeare.

Joan of Arc and Queen Elizabeth were two strong women who had a huge impact on the times in which they lived. Write a two to three-page paper that compares the two women and speaks to the shared traits that made them impactful, besides being strong women.

Columbus discovers San Salvador in 1492, and Copernicus' model of a sun-centered universe is revealed (1530). Michaelangelo (Michelangelo), the architect of St. Peter's and so much more, is found at year A.D. 1474. The painter Raphael (1483) is shown in red just above the word "OTTOMAN" in "OTTOMAN-EMPIRE."

Archbishop James Ussher (Usher as spelled by Adams) is born in 1581. Living to the age of 80, he will author *The Annals of World History,* one of but many works consulted in the creation of this time-line.

Twentieth Panel: A.D. 1600 to 1878

The "United States of America" is featured prominently at the top in this, the next to last panel of Adams' time-line. To the left side of the panel, above the "Stream of Time," we see pictured the ruins of the Stone Church at Jamestown, Virginia, the authorized "Holy Bible, King James" version, the first newspaper, Galileo's telescope and thermometer, Sir Isaac Newton under the apple tree, the first balloon, Ben Franklin flying a kite, the first mail coaches, Jas. Watt and the power of steam, the monument to commemorate the Battle of Bunker Hill, Daguerre's camera, the Book of Mormon, and the first telegraph line, passenger steamboat, and railroad.

Below the "Stream of Time" and looking down the left side, we see that Galileo has as contemporaries Francis Bacon, John Milton (poet), Archbishop Ussher, and Murillo (Spanish painter). From top to bottom are Addison, Newton, Locke, William Penn, and Spinozza. And Ben Franklin, Robert Burns, Gibbon, Goldsmith, Blackstone, Hume Handel (George), Voltaire, Cowper, Mozart, Herschel, and Beethoven are all contemporaries, or nearly so.

The power of Spain begins to erode in 1640 when Philip IV loses Portugal, California, Gibraltar, Maples and Sicily, Florida, and finally Argentina, Columbia, Chile, Peru, and Mexico. Portugal splits off Brazil. Greece gains independence from the Ottoman Empire/Turkey in 1830. Germany is fragmented. Small nation-states with their own rulers, nations like Baden and Wurtemberg (see upper right under "stream of time") Bavaria, and Saxony strive to exist and co-exist at the end of the 1870s.

The Last (or Twenty-first) Panel:

At the top of the chart are the presidents of the United States through the 19th, Rutherford B. Hayes. Notice the numbers at the top of each illustrated president. Washington is #1 and, above Hayes, #19. These small numerals depict the order of the presidents. Below each illustration are the birth and death dates of the presidents. Between are the years the person lived. For Washington this was 67 years.

Complete the list of all presidents up to the current one; include their birthdays and dates of their demise, where applicable.

What president among those illustrated on the Chart lived the longest?

Who among all presidents has lived the longest?

How do the ages compare to Adam and Noah's years on earth?

How many states were there in 1878?

Below the illustrated presidents of the United States are two columns of drawings with captions. The columns are labeled "The Past" and "The Present," the present, in this case, being the 1870s. The 14 illustrations of Past/Present cover seven different ways or areas of human advancement.

What are the seven areas Adams chooses to show had advanced?

Have we advanced beyond Adams' Present?

Identify the following people, inventions, or events: Columbus; S.F.B. Morse; Elias Howel; Spinning Jenny; "The last spike driven, May 10, 1869"; Geneva Council, September 14, 1872.

Which of these would you deem most important? Why?

To the immediate left of the first panel under "The Past" are two names, H. Clay and Daniel Webster, and a heading that says, "United States with Alaska." Notice the additional information given for the individuals and the nation. Was Alaska a state in 1878?

THE "ATLANTIC TELEGRAPH CABLE" FROM ENG. TO AM.CA. NOW IN OPERATION. WAS COMPLETED, JULY 27.th 1867. ORGINAL PROJECTORS S.F.B. MORSE, CYRUS W. FIELD. ETC.

Who are H. Clay and Daniel Webster?

What had they done that made them worthy of becoming a "salient fact" in Adams' Chart?

According to the Chart, what was the population of the United States?

List the current rulers that are illustrated under the United States, starting with Queen Victoria of Great Britain.

Of the countries listed vertically beside the illustrations of "The Past," what rulers are not pictured?

Where is "Hanover" located?

In Conclusion
The possibilities are endless. The more you make use of the time-line, the more your knowledge will grow. Adams has given an illustrated framework for understanding the big picture and comprehending vast amounts of knowledge.

We welcome any comments or suggestions. If you are finding new ways to use the chart, please let us know so we may share with others. Contact Master Books at www.masterbooks.net. Thank you!

Appendix A: Higher Order Thinking Skills (H.O.T.S.) of Bloom's Taxonomy

IV: Progressive Levels of Learning: Using Bloom's Taxonomy	Skills	Ask questions that ask you to....
Evaluation / Synthesis / Analysis / Application / Understanding / Knowledge (pyramid diagram)	Knowledge:	arrange, define, duplicate, label, list, memorize, name, order, recognize, relate, recall, repeat, reproduce, state, tell, describe, locate, write, find, identify, show, collect, examine, tabulate, quote, who, when, where.
	Comprehension:	classify, describe, discuss, explain, express, identify, indicate, locate, recognize, report, restate, review, select, translate, interpret, outline, distinguish, predict, compare, summarize, contrast, associate, estimate, differentiate, extend.
	Application:	apply, choose, demonstrate, dramatize, employ, illustrate, interpret, operate, practice, schedule, sketch, solve, use, write, show, construct, complete, examine, classify, calculate, modify, relate, change, experiment, discover.
	Analysis:	analyze, appraise, calculate, categorize, compare, contrast, criticize, differentiate, discriminate, distinguish, examine, experiment, question, test, investigate, identify, explain, separate, advertise, order, connect, classify, arrange, divide, select, infer.
	Synthesis:	arrange, assemble, collect, compose, construct, create, design, develop, formulate, manage, organize, plan, prepare, propose, set up, write, create, invent, predict, imagine, devise, combine, integrate, modify, rearrange, substitute, generalize, rewrite.
	Evaluation:	appraise, argue, assess, attach, choose, compare, defend, estimate, judge, predict, rate, core, select, support, value, evaluate, decide, justify, debate, verify, discuss, prioritize, determine, rank, grade, test, measure, recommend, convince, explain, discriminate, conclude, summarize.

Using Bloom's Taxonomy of Learning can help your explorer engage learning from facts to using higher order thinking skills. It's a key element to strong learning. Bloom divided learning into levels, starting with Knowledge and Comprehension (of content) to Higher Order Thinking Skills (HOTS) such as Analysis, Synthesis, and Evaluation. By asking questions and developing activities using all the different levels of Bloom's Taxonomy, you should be able to present information at appropriate levels for your youngest to your oldest. Please be sure to include the questions that your child asks! Their questions will serve as your guide to where they are on the taxonomy.

As teachers, we tend to ask questions in the "knowledge" category 80 to 90 percent of the time. These questions are not bad, but using them all the time is. Try to utilize higher-order level questions. These questions require much more "brain power" and a more extensive and elaborate answer. The chart shows the six question categories as defined by Bloom.

Remembering; memorizing; recognizing; recalling; identification; and recall of information
» Who, what, when, where, how ...?
» Describe

Interpreting; translating from one medium to another; describing in one's own words; organization and selection of facts and ideas
» Retell...
» Summarize the main point, in the correct order
» What was the problem – how was it solved
» Predict how the story will end

FACT FOUNDATION

Problem solving; applying information to produce some result; use of facts, rules, and principles
» How is...an example of...?
» How is...related to...?
» Why is...significant?

Subdividing something to show how it is put together; finding the underlying structure of a communication; identifying motives; separation of a whole into component parts
» What are the parts or features of...?
» Classify...according to...
» Outline/diagram...
» How does...compare/contrast with...?
» What evidence can you list for...?

Creating a unique, original product that may be in verbal form or may be a physical object; combination of ideas to form a new whole
» What would you predict/infer from...?
» What ideas can you add to...?
» How would you create/design a new...?
» What might happen if you combined...?
» What solutions would you suggest for...?

Making value decisions about issues; resolving controversies or differences of opinion; development of opinions, judgments, or decisions
» Do you agree...?
» What do you think about...?
» What is the most important...?
» Place the following in order of priority...
» How would you decide about...?
» What criteria would you use to assess...?

HIGHER ORDER THINKING SKILLS

TESTS

These tests are intended to be open chart/book. Factual information needs repetition to help retention. Follow up short answer or essay tests (provided) are intended to check higher order thinking skills for older students/adults.

MATCHING

_____1. Adam   A. 980 B.C.

_____2. Alexander the Great   B. A.D. 1732

_____3. Attila the Hun   C. 4004 B.C.

_____4. J. Caesar   D. A.D. 1500

_____5. Jesus Christ   E. 360 B.C

_____6. Copernicus   F. A.D. 1789

_____7. Benjamin Franklin   G. 580 B.C.

_____8. Homer   H. 70 B.C.

_____9. Nebuchadnezzar   I. A.D. 33

_____10. George Washington   J. A.D. 424

MULTIPLE CHOICE

_____ 1. Who was a mathematician?

      a. Franklin

      b. Shem

      c. Copernicus

      d. Alexander

_____ 2. Another name for the Deluge is_____

      a. the Landing

      b. the Fire

      c. the Earthquake

      d. the Flood

_____ 3. The ruler who built the Tower of Babel was_____

      a. Nimrod

      b. Caesar

      c. Alexander the Great

      d. Nebchadnezzar

_____ 4. Who developed a working printing press?

      a. Franklin

      b. Guttenberg

      c. Ptolemy

      d. Luther

_____ 5. Who was burned at the stake?

      a. Isabella of Spain

      b. Anne of Fayette

      c. Eve

      d. Joan of Arc

_____ 6. The First Crusade was in the year_____

      a. A.D. 1096

      b. 469 B.C.

      c. A.D. 1492

      d. A.D. 496

_____ 7. Noah had three sons: Ham, Shem and_____

      a. Jubal

      b. Lamech

      c. Japheth

      d. Levi

_____ 8. The 7 Wonders of the World (given on the chart) included all but_____

        a. the Pyramids

        b. the Mausoleum

        c. Babylon

        d. the Coliseum

_____ 9. The center of the Ptolemaic System is the_____

        a. earth

        b. sun

        c. moon

        d. ocean

_____ 10. What was the sacred chest where "The Law" only was deposited?

        a. Alter of Incense

        b. Table of Shewbread

        c. Ark of the Covenant

        d. Brazen Laver for Sacred Ablutions

TRUE/FALSE

Circle "T" if you believe the statement to be true. Circle "F" if you believe the statement to be false. Correct the false statements to make them true.

T F   1. The chart depicts the rise of nations developing after the Tower of Babel.

T F   2. Ben Franklin developed the German alphabet.

T F   3. The Persian Empire grew to include Egypt, Babylon, and Media.

T F   4. Methuselah lived to be 1,069 years of age.

T F   5. Socrates died by drinking hemlock.

T F   6. At the time of Jesus' death, Tiberius was Caesar of the Roman Empire.

T F   7. Galileo invented the microscope in A.D. 1610.

T F   8. The first passenger steamboat (1807) was the Hudson on the Clermont River.

T F   9. Constantine the Great was the first Christian emperor of the Roman Empire.

T F   10. Eratosthenes conceived of the plan to measure the earth's circumference.

FILL IN THE BLANK

1. Born around 287 B.C. and generally regarded as the greatest mathematician and scientist of antiquity, _____ used his math ability to make war machines and a water screw.

2. The Ecumenical Council formed the _____ _____ in A.D. 325.

3. Queen Elizabeth (A.D. 1558) of England was the daughter of _____ _____.

4. Traveling by wagon took six months to go 2,000 miles; by train in 1870 a distance of 3,200 miles could be covered in only _____ days.

5. According to the illustration beneath "The Deluge," the ark weighed _____ tons.

6. Adam passed the history of his time to Methuselah, who passed it on to Noah's son _____.

7. Much of the history and works of antiquity were lost with the burning of the library at _____.

8. The _____ Stone, with the same message written in three languages, provided the key to decipher the hieroglyphics of ancient Egypt.

9. The second Book of Samuel covers from _____ B.C. to _____ B.C.

10. Looking around A.D. 500, the new nation-state of Scandinavia becomes three nations by A.D. 800: _____, _____ and _____.

SHORT ANSWER QUESTIONS

Using the chart, complete the following.

1. Compare and contrast the Persian Empire and the Roman Empire.

2. Of all the inventions illustrated on the chart, choose your top three and explain why you rank them 1, 2, and 3.

3. Of all the architecture illustrated on the chart, which is the most different? Why?

4. Adam lived 960 years, Methuselah lived 969, yet after Noah's Deluge in 2348 B.C. people started living shorter and shorter life spans. Why do you think this is so?

5. The chart ends at 1878 A.D. Below the Presidents of the United States is an illustration entitled "The Past — The Present." Using what you know or can research, make your own panels for "The Present." Let Adams' "The Present" become your "The Past."

ANSWER KEY

MATCHING

__C__	1. Adam		A.	980 B.C.
__E__	2. Alexander the Great		B.	A.D. 1732
__J__	3. Attila the Hun		C.	4004 B.C.
__H__	4. J. Caesar		D.	A.D. 1500
__I__	5. Jesus Christ		E.	360 B.C
__D__	6. Copernicus		F.	A.D.1789
__B__	7. Benjamin Franklin		G.	580 B.C.
__A__	8. Homer A		H.	70 B.C.
__G__	9. Nebuchadnezzar		I.	A.D. 33
__F__	10. George Washington		J.	A.D. 424

MULTIPLE CHOICE

__C__ 1. Who was a mathematician?

    a. Franklin

    b. Shem

    c. Copernicus

    d. Alexander

__D__ 2. Another name for the Deluge is?

    a. the Landing

    b. the Fire

    c. the Earthquake

    d. the Flood

__A__ 3. The ruler who built the Tower of Babel was?

    a. Nimrod

    b. Caesar

    c. Alexander the Great

    d. Nebchadnezzar

__B__ 4. Who developed a working printing press?

    a. Franklin

    b. Guttenberg

    c. Ptolemy

    d. Luther

__D__ 5. Who was burned at the stake?

        a. Isabella of Spain

        b. Anne of Fayette

        c. Eve

        d. Joan of Arc

__A__ 6. The First Crusade was in the year?

        a. A.D. 1096

        b. 469 B.C.

        c. A.D. 1492

        d. A.D. 496

__C__ 7. Noah had three sons. Ham, Shem, and?

        a. Jubal

        b. Lamech

        c. Japheth

        d. Levi

__D__ 8. The 7 Wonders of the World (given on the chart) included all but?

        a. the Pyramids

        b. the Mausoleum

        c. Babylon

        d. the Coliseum

__A__ 9. The center of the Ptolemaic System is the?

        a. earth

        b. sun

        c. moon

        d. ocean

__C__ 10. What was the sacred chest where "The Law" only was deposited?

        a. Alter of Incense

        b. Table of Shewbread

        c. Ark of the Covenant

        d. Brazen Laver for Sacred Ablutions

TRUE/FALSE

1. T
2. F
3. T
4. F
5. T
6. T
7. F
8. F
9. T
10. T

FILL IN THE BLANK

1. Archimedes
2. Nicene Creed
3. Anne Boleyn
4. six
5. 81,000
6. Shem
7. Alexandria
8. Rosetta
9. 1055 B.C. to 1017 B.C.
10. Sweden, Denmark, and Norway

SHORT ANSWER QUESTIONS

The answers will vary greatly for this section of the assessment. This is as it should be. The purpose of this section is to provoke deeper thinking. The results may be one's opinion, yet the answers should be defensible based on fact, logic, or reason. This assessment definitely engages the higher order thinking skills of Bloom's Taxonomy of Learning. Students will need to Analyze (take apart), Synthesize (put together), and Evaluate (judge) in order to answer these questions.

Please be sure to set aside ample time for in-depth discussion of these questions. It may be that you want to discuss only one per day.

Adams' Chart of History

Sebastian Adams

Discover:

• Who were the first navigators?
• Who was the Emperor of China during the reign of Solomon?
• What kinds of alphabets were used in the ancient world?
• What advances in mathematics were being made while Nebuchadnezzar was reigning?
• How much was the Bible worth in 1440 AD?

Study

• Timeline includes detailed biblical history
• Ancient history (including Greek and Roman)
• Inventions, Discoveries, and Events
• European and American early history, and many other details

One-of-a-kind:

• Based on Archibishop James Ussher's classic work, *The Annals of the World*
• 21 full-color panels, large format time-line that is easy to read — nothing on the market this size.
• Starts with creation at 4004 B.C. and goes to 1870 and our 19th president R.B. Hayes

Sebastian Adams, in early as in later life, was a studious and earnest scholar. The son of a prominent family who were patrons of education and science, he would become an educator, statesman, and author during his lifetime of achievements. It was from his mother that he developed his love for research and the perseverance to create this incomparable time-line of history.

Included with this beautiful chart of history, is the 60-page key of the original 1871 time-line.

This thorough and fascinating key is a guide for how to teach from the time-line and expands on the history of the different cultures and countries covered in the time-line, from Macedonia, to Egypt, to the United States. This great added resource will help you get the most from your time-line — whether for Christian education, general interest, or ministerial applications.